EYEWITNESS TO HISTORY

HARRIET TUBMAN

in her own words

Gareth Stevens
PUBLISHING

By Julia McDonnell

Please visit our website, www.garethstevens.com. For a free color catalog of all our high-quality books, call toll free 1-800-542-2595 or fax 1-877-542-2596.

Library of Congress Cataloging-in-Publication Data

McDonnell, Julia, 1979-
 Harriet Tubman in her own words / Julia McDonnell.
    pages cm. — (Eyewitness to history)
 Includes index.
 ISBN 978-1-4824-4066-9 (pbk.)
 ISBN 978-1-4824-4068-3 (6 pack)
 ISBN 978-1-4824-4067-6 (library binding)
 1. Tubman, Harriet, 1820?-1913—Juvenile literature. 2. Slaves—United States—Biography Juvenile literature. 3. African American women—Biography—Juvenile literature. 4. Underground Railroad—Juvenile literature. 5. Antislavery movements—United States—History—19th century—Juvenile literature. I. Title.
 E444.T82M373 2015
 973.7115092—dc23
 [B]

                                        2015030538

First Edition

Published in 2016 by
Gareth Stevens Publishing
111 East 14th Street, Suite 349
New York, NY 10003

Copyright © 2016 Gareth Stevens Publishing

Designer: Katelyn E. Reynolds
Editor: Therese Shea

Photo credits: Cover, p. 1 (Harriet Tubman) Library of Congress/Wikipedia.org; cover, pp. 1 (background image), 5, 20 Wikipedia.org; cover, p. 1 (logo quill icon) Seamartini Graphics Media/Shutterstock.com; cover, p. 1 (logo stamp) YasnaTen/Shutterstock.com; cover, p. 1 (color grunge frame) DmitryPrudnichenko/Shutterstock.com; cover, pp. 1–32 (paper background) Nella/Shutterstock.com; cover, pp. 1–32 (decorative elements) Ozerina Anna/Shutterstock.com; pp. 1–32 (wood texture) Reinhold Leitner/Shutterstock.com; pp. 1–32 (open book background) Elena Schweitzer/Shutterstock.com; pp. 1–32 (bookmark) Robert Adrian Hillman/Shutterstock.com; pp. 4, 15, 25 Everett Historical/Shutterstock.com; pp. 7, 13 Hulton Archive/Getty Images; p. 9 Jupiterimages/Stockbyte/Getty Images; pp. 10–11 MPI/Getty Images; pp. 16–17 Cincinnati Art Museum/Wikipedia.org; pp. 19, 21 courtesy of the Library of Congress; p. 23 LouLouPhotos/Shutterstock.com; p. 25 (signature) U.S. House of Representatives/Wikipedia.org; p. 27 Ann Ronan Pictures/Print Collector/Getty Images; p. 28 stockelements/Shutterstock.com.

Printed in the United States of America

CPSIA compliance information: Batch #CW16GS: For further information contact Gareth Stevens, New York, New York at 1-800-542-2595.

CONTENTS

*Words in the glossary appear in **bold** type the first time they are used in the text.*

An UNLIKELY Hero

MORE TO KNOW

Tubman's name at birth was Araminta Harriet Ross. She was called "Minty" as a child but later went by "Harriet" because it was her mother's name.

European **immigrants** settled in the territory that became the United States in search of religious freedom and economic opportunity. However, some of the earliest Americans didn't arrive by choice. Many were Africans who were sold as slaves and forced to work for white masters. Some brave individuals risked their life to help them escape.

Harriet Tubman never learned to read or write. When writer Sarah Bradford began a biography of Tubman, she interviewed her and gathered others' accounts of her deeds. Many of Tubman's quotes in this book are taken from that biography—*Harriet Tubman: The Moses of Her People*. Bradford wrote down Tubman's words phonetically, which means she used unusual spelling to reflect what Tubman sounded like. In this book, these quotes are presented as close as possible to those in Bradford's biography, while making them easier for modern readers to understand.

One of these was Harriet Tubman, who had been a slave herself and understood the desperation for freedom. Tubman once said, *"I've seen hundreds and hundreds of slaves who finally got to the North and freedom. But I never yet saw one who was willing to go back South and be a slave."* Small in size, suffering from poor health, and lacking an education, she nevertheless became one of the most famous Americans in history.

BORN INTO *Hardship*

FAMILY DEVOTION

Slave owners usually didn't care whether they split up parents, children, and siblings when selling and trading their workers. However, the bonds of the Ross family remained strong despite separation. Tubman eventually rescued siblings, nieces, nephews, and her elderly parents. They worked together to keep each other safe by communicating in code, sneaking food to those who were in hiding, and wearing blindfolds so they could claim they didn't see anyone trying to escape.

Harriet Tubman was born sometime in 1820 or 1821 along the Big Buckwater River near Bucktown, Maryland. Her grandparents had come from west Africa, slaves before they even arrived on American soil. Tubman's parents, Benjamin "Old Ben" Ross and Harriet "Rit" Greene, were owned by Edward Brodess, whose farm produced corn, rye, and wheat as well as timber.

Tubman spent her early years being cared for by older slave women. From a young age, she dreamed of freedom, imagining herself flying over the land and reaching a river—*"but it appeared like I wouldn't have the strength [to get across], and just as I was sinking down, there would be ladies . . . and they would put out their arms and pull me 'cross."*

The Mason-Dixon line was the official border separating Maryland, Pennsylvania, and Delaware. It was also the symbolic boundary between the free North and the slave South. Bucktown was only about 100 miles (160 km) from Pennsylvania.

Slaves usually lived in small, crowded cabins on their master's property.

All WORK

At the age of 3, Harriet Tubman was put to work. She ran errands and carried messages, often for distances of several miles. By the time she was 6, Tubman was sent to nearby families who paid her owner for services such as weaving, checking animal traps, housekeeping, and caring for babies.

These people treated Tubman just as harshly as her master did. As a result, she often became sick and couldn't fulfill her responsibilities. Sometimes, she was whipped as punishment. Feeling alone, Tubman often turned to religion to get through difficulties. She said, *"I prayed all the time about my work, everywhere; I was always talking to the Lord."* As a teenager, she began to work in the fields as a farm laborer.

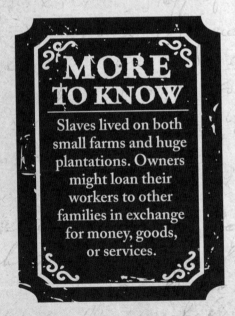

MORE TO KNOW

Slaves lived on both small farms and huge plantations. Owners might loan their workers to other families in exchange for money, goods, or services.

Many slaves in the South worked in cotton fields. It was hard, hot, and exhausting labor.

FREE ALL ALONG?

Years later, Tubman hired a lawyer to research her family's background. She learned her mother's master's will had ordered that the older Tubman be given to his granddaughter Mary Patterson, but receive her freedom upon turning 45. Patterson's early death meant Tubman's mother was sold instead, and the will's instructions were forgotten. Tubman's mother was likely free under the law, but no one ever told her. She and her children remained slaves until they escaped.

A VICTIM OF *Cruelty*

AN UNEXPECTED GIFT

Tubman repeatedly had a dream featuring an older bearded man and two younger men being attacked by a mob. In 1858, she met the abolitionist John Brown, who she said looked exactly like the man in her vision. He tried to begin a slave uprising in October 1859. On that day, Tubman had no knowledge of his plan, but insisted she felt a warning about Brown. His two sons were killed, and he was executed soon after. She believed she had predicted their deaths.

In 1835, a life-changing event happened. Tubman was in a store when another field slave suddenly dashed in, trying to escape an overseer. The overseer caught the slave and ordered Tubman to hold the runaway while he tied him up. Tubman refused, the man bolted away, and the overseer

threw a heavy lead weight to try to stop him. It hit Tubman in the forehead instead, leaving her **unconscious** for days and with a permanent scar. The blow affected her for the rest of her life, bringing on unexpected sleeping spells, painful headaches, and visions.

The brutality and inequality of slavery became even clearer to Tubman. But her kind nature remained: *"I was always praying for poor old master . . . . 'Oh, dear Lord, change that man's heart.'"*

MORE TO KNOW

In 2015, the American public was asked to vote for the woman they would like to see on a redesigned $20 bill. Tubman was chosen over 14 other candidates.

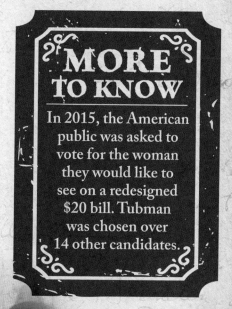

Tubman is shown here (far left) with friends and family members at her home in Auburn, New York, in 1887.

11

ALWAYS *Uneasy*

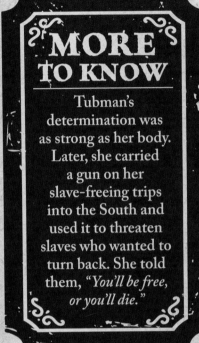

MORE TO KNOW

Tubman's determination was as strong as her body. Later, she carried a gun on her slave-freeing trips into the South and used it to threaten slaves who wanted to turn back. She told them, *"You'll be free, or you'll die."*

Despite her injury, Tubman's reputation as a capable field worker grew. She lived in fear of being sold farther South, so she performed her tasks as well as she could. Tubman's request to work on her father's lumber-cutting crew was approved, and she did such a good job that she was allowed to hire herself out to other families and keep most of the wages she earned.

Though Tubman's treatment was slightly better than that of other slaves, she still wanted more freedom and security: *"I grew up like a weed—ignorant of liberty, having no experience of it . . . I was not happy or contented. Every time I saw a white man I was afraid of being carried away. We were always uneasy."*

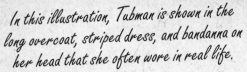

In this illustration, Tubman is shown in the long overcoat, striped dress, and bandanna on her head that she often wore in real life.

HARD WORK AND HUMILIATION

Tubman became known for her strength. Despite being only 5 feet (1.5 m) tall, she could perform the same work as a man. She plowed and planted crops, drove oxen, loaded wagons, and chopped wood. But sometimes those valuable skills brought her unwanted attention. Her master had her perform for guests, **hitching** her to a boat and loading it with heavy stones. She was made to walk along the riverbank, pulling the boat upstream and amazing spectators with her physical abilities.

A LIFE-CHANGING Decision

SECRETS IN SONGS

Harriet wanted her friends and family to know that she was leaving, but she couldn't risk the wrong people discovering her plan. So she paid them a visit and sang a song that included these lines: *"I'm sorry I'm going to leave you"* and *"I'll meet you in the morning / I'm bound for the Promised Land."* Slaves often passed messages to each other through hymns. Most listeners weren't suspicious of religious songs.

Harriet gained more independence when she married John Tubman, a free black man, in 1844. She shared a home with him, and this taste of freedom convinced her that she couldn't spend the rest of her life in slavery. But her husband was happy with the way things were, and he threatened to tell her master if she tried to leave.

By 1849, Harriet couldn't wait any longer. Two of her sisters had just been sold, and she feared she'd be next: *"I heard that . . . I was to be sent with my brothers in the chain-gang to the far South."* The fear of being sent away from her family to likely face even harsher punishment than in Maryland prompted her to leave.

MORE TO KNOW

Runaway slaves used nature to point them toward freedom. The side of a tree trunk that moss grew on, the direction of migrating birds and flowing rivers, and the North Star's location were the types of clues they looked for.

Some slaves escaped in creative ways. In 1856, Henry Brown had himself packed into a shipping crate and mailed from Virginia to Pennsylvania!

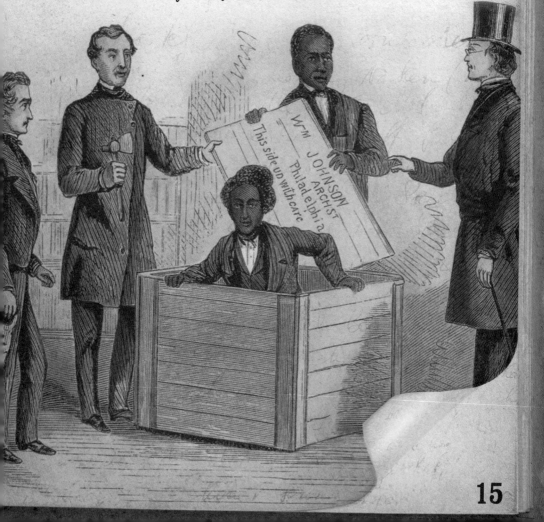

FREEDOM
at Last

Traveling at night was safer, so Harriet left after John was asleep. She had heard that a white woman in Bucktown would help runaways, so she nervously knocked on her door. Welcomed into the home, the woman gave Harriet instructions on where to go and whom to see on her journey.

With the help of several people sympathetic to slaves, Harriet passed through Maryland and Delaware, hiding in wagons or in plain sight

> ### MORE TO KNOW
>
> The Underground Railroad supposedly got its name when runaway slave Tice Davids seemed to disappear after crossing the Ohio River. His master is said to have remarked, *"He must have gone on an underground road."*

while acting as if she was another family's slave. She eventually reached Pennsylvania—and freedom.
In that moment, she said, *"I looked at my hands to see if I was the same person now I was free. There was such a glory over everything . . . I felt like I was in Heaven."*

Runaways risked bad weather, hunting dogs, armed slave catchers, dangers in nature, and betrayals in their attempts to reach freedom. They had to trust guides and strangers or try to make the journey on their own.

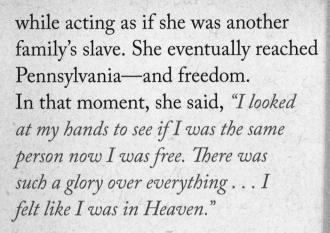

A RAILROAD WITH NO TRAINS

The Underground Railroad was an organized network of people committed to helping runaway slaves reach freedom. It had nothing to do with trains, but it did use similar terms. A "station" or "junction" was a safe place in which to hide. People involved were known as "agents," "conductors," or "station masters." The runaway slaves were "passengers" or "parcels." And it had "lines" that traveled through Ohio, Indiana, Pennsylvania, New Jersey, and other states.

Finding a New PURPOSE

Harriet Tubman stayed in Philadelphia, working in a hotel kitchen. She was lonely, so she became involved in antislavery groups like the Vigilance Committee, which provided runaway slaves with food and shelter. Soon, she was given the opportunity to guide people to freedom when a man asked for help rescuing a woman and her children from Maryland. Tubman listened to his story and realized he was talking about her own family! She insisted on taking the mission, later saying, *"My home, after all, was down in the old cabin quarter [in Maryland], with the old folks, and my brothers and sisters . . . They should be free also."*

Once the Underground Railroad brought her family to Baltimore, Tubman led them into Pennsylvania and freedom. Other trips soon followed.

PARTNERS IN THE FIGHT

Abolitionists were people who believed slavery and **racism** were wrong. They organized themselves into a movement in the 1830s. They published newspapers, gave speeches, and tried to get laws passed making slavery illegal. Many people joined the cause, despite it often being dangerous. Abolitionist William Lloyd Garrison was almost killed by an angry mob because of his writings. Abolitionists were whites, blacks, men, and women who worked together and saw each other as equals, which was rare at that time.

Quakers were members of a Christian church who helped operate the Underground Railroad, hiding runaways and raising funds. Tubman said, *"Quakers . . . call themselves friends and you can trust them every time."*

Owners advertised rewards for their runaway slaves, sharing descriptions in the hope that someone would recognize them and turn them in.

$150 REWARD

RANAWAY from the subscriber, on the night of the 2d instant, a negro man, who calls himself *Henry May*, about 22 years old, 5 feet 6 or 8 inches high, ordinary color, rather chunky built, bushy head, and has it divided mostly on one side, and keeps it very nicely combed; has been raised in the house, and is a first rate dining-room servant, and was in a tavern in Louisville for 18 months. I expect he is now in Louisville trying to make his escape to a free state, (in all probability to Cincinnati, Ohio.) Perhaps he may try to get employment on a steamboat. He is a good cook, and is handy in any capacity as a house servant. Had on when he left, a dark cassinett coatee, and dark striped cassinett pantaloons, new---he had other clothing. I will give $50 reward if taken in Louisvill; 100 dollars if tak[en] one hundred miles from Louisville in this State, and 150 [dollars if taken out] of this State, and delivered to me, or secured in any jai[l] [so that I can get him] again.

WIL[LIAM BURKE]

Bardstown, Ky., September 3d, 1838.

TAKING ACTION,
Taking Risks

When laws became harsher toward runaway slaves (and the people who helped them) in 1850, Tubman changed her destination. *"I wouldn't trust Uncle Sam with my people no longer, but I brought 'em all clear off to Canada,"* she said.

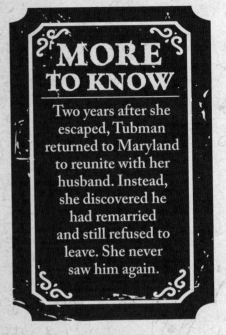

MORE TO KNOW

Two years after she escaped, Tubman returned to Maryland to reunite with her husband. Instead, she discovered he had remarried and still refused to leave. She never saw him again.

Smaller branches of the Underground Railroad joined up with established main routes that led to freedom in the North.

ROUTES OF THE
UNDERGROUND
RAILROAD
1850 - 1865

Compiled from "The Underground Railroad from Slavery to Freedom" By Wilbur H. Siebert. Copyright, 1898, by The Macmillan Company.

She used a 650-mile (1,050 km) route between Maryland and the Canadian city of St. Catharines and worked as a cook and housekeeper in New Jersey during summer. The pay funded the two trips she made each year, guiding slaves along the Underground Railroad.

When Tubman reflected on her many successful rescues, she remarked, *"I can say what most conductors can't say—I never ran my train off the track and I never lost a passenger."* And she was finally able to lead her parents to freedom in 1857.

THE MOSES OF HER PEOPLE

Tubman was called "Moses" by slaves, after the figure in the Bible who led his people out of slavery under the Egyptians. Slaves compared their long, forbidden journey through unfamiliar and dangerous territory toward a "promised land" in the North to the journey the Israelites took thousands of years before. Soon whites and blacks, Northerners and Southerners, were using the name for her as well.

DARING *Rescue*

A SHARP MIND

Tubman's ability to think quickly saved her life many times. Once, while at a railroad station in the South, she saw a poster with her picture offering a reward for her capture. She heard two men arguing whether she was the person in the poster. She opened a book she was carrying and fooled them into thinking she was reading. Since it was correctly believed that Harriet Tubman couldn't read, they left her alone.

Harriet Tubman moved to Auburn, New York, in 1857 and began working closely with fellow abolitionists. Her passionate speeches drew large audiences. However, she was still willing to undertake dangerous missions.

In 1860, a slave named Charles Nalle was caught in Troy, New York, and ordered to be returned to his master. Tubman led a crowd that grabbed him from his guards. Shielding him with her own body, she cried, *"Drag us out! Drag him to the river! Drown him! But don't let them have him!"*

Two men were shot in the struggle, but Nalle was **smuggled** into Canada in a wagon. Tubman had to go into hiding. She became convinced

that slavery couldn't be ended without violence:
"They may say, 'Peace, Peace' as much as they likes, I know it's going to be war."

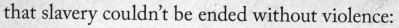

The Gateway to Freedom statue shows several slaves being guided across the Detroit River to liberty in Windsor, Canada.

MORE TO KNOW

One of Tubman's tricks was to plan her escapes on Saturday nights, since Sunday was a day of rest. She hoped no one would notice the slaves were missing until Monday morning.

GENERAL *Tubman*

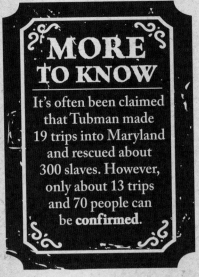
Harriet Tubman was right: a civil war between Northern and Southern states began in 1861. She was asked to help the many slaves who were abandoned by their masters and left hungry and homeless. She also served as a nurse to **Union** soldiers and even led bands of black troops on scouting missions. Abolitionist John Brown had once called Harriet "General Tubman" because she was such a capable leader. Her actions during the Civil War proved this.

Tubman found herself close to battle: *"We saw the lightning, and that was the guns; and then we heard thunder, and that was the big guns; and then we heard the rain falling, and that was drops of blood falling, and when we came to get in the crops, it was dead men that we **reaped**."*

Harriet Tubman's actual signature:

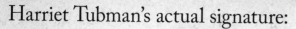

The 54th Massachusetts Volunteer Infantry, a group of free black soldiers, famously attacked South Carolina's Fort Wagner in July 1863. Tubman cared for the injured survivors.

COMBAHEE RIVER RAID

Tubman was the only woman to plan and lead a military operation during the American Civil War. Under her guidance, three Union gunboats manned by black soldiers traveled down South Carolina's Combahee River, burning plantations and gathering supplies. Local slaves raced to the riverbank and were encouraged by Tubman to board the vessels. Confederate forces were caught off guard. It was an overwhelming victory for the North, and over 700 slaves were set free.

ALWAYS
Serving Others

UNSHAKABLE FAITH

Thomas Garrett, an Underground Railroad conductor, said, *"I never met with any person, of any color, who had more **confidence** in the voice of God."* Tubman believed visions she experienced carried **divine** messages and was sure her prayers were heard. She didn't take credit for much, saying, *"It wasn't me; 'twas the Lord! Just so long as he wanted to use me, he would take care of me . . . I always told him, 'I'm going to hold steady onto you, and you've got to see me through.'"*

After the North won the war and slaves were **emancipated**, Harriet Tubman returned to Auburn. She shared what little money she had with anyone who needed it. She still had the energy and drive to support her causes, which included women's **suffrage** and education for black children. She also founded a home for the needy, sick, and poor. Tubman moved into that facility, the Harriet Tubman Home, in 1911 and stayed until her death on March 10, 1913.

Tubman's work had achieved liberty for herself and for countless others. Social reformer Gerrit Smith wrote of her, *"Nearly all the nation over, [Harriet Tubman] has been heard of for her wisdom, **integrity**, patriotism, and bravery. The cause of freedom owes her much. The country owes her much."*

This photo, taken around 1913, shows Harriet in her 90s.

A LEGACY
That Inspires

MORE TO KNOW

Queen Victoria of England awarded Tubman a silver medal and sent her a personal letter.

The nation hasn't forgotten Harriet Tubman. Many schools, buildings, and memorials carry her name. Learning centers and museums educate visitors about her incredible story. Tubman was the first African American woman honored with an official US stamp. Underground Railroad sites have been preserved in her honor. And shelters and hospitals for the needy continue the efforts she began late in life, which she called her *"last work."*

Tubman's life is truly remarkable: She was a slave, runaway, abolitionist, spy, nurse, women's rights activist, and education supporter. Rising from humble slave beginnings to become one of the most courageous and generous women of her time, her work continues to inspire people today.

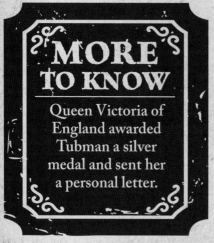

A statue of Harriet Tubman stands in the Harlem section of New York City.

TIMELINE
HARRIET TUBMAN'S LIFE

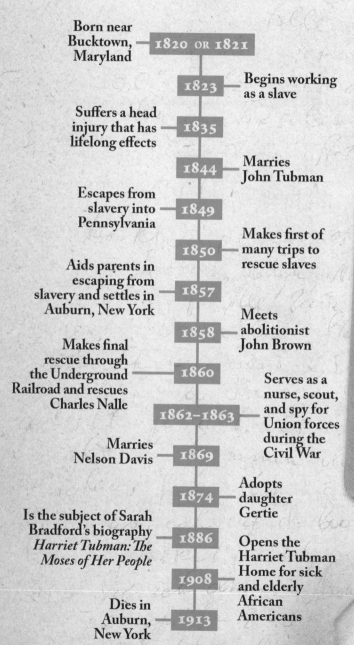

Born near Bucktown, Maryland — **1820 or 1821**

1823 — Begins working as a slave

Suffers a head injury that has lifelong effects — **1835**

1844 — Marries John Tubman

Escapes from slavery into Pennsylvania — **1849**

1850 — Makes first of many trips to rescue slaves

Aids parents in escaping from slavery and settles in Auburn, New York — **1857**

1858 — Meets abolitionist John Brown

Makes final rescue through the Underground Railroad and rescues Charles Nalle — **1860**

1862–1863 — Serves as a nurse, scout, and spy for Union forces during the Civil War

Marries Nelson Davis — **1869**

1874 — Adopts daughter Gertie

Is the subject of Sarah Bradford's biography *Harriet Tubman: The Moses of Her People* — **1886**

1886 — Opens the Harriet Tubman Home for sick and elderly African Americans

1908

Dies in Auburn, New York — **1913**

STUBBORN TO THE LAST

Tubman often used her mind—and her stubbornness—to accomplish things. When she needed money to establish her home for elderly and disabled African Americans, she asked others to contribute. On one occasion, she visited a certain man to ask him for $20. Beforehand, she said, *"I ain't going to leave there, and I ain't going to eat or drink, till I get money enough."* At first, the man refused. So Tubman sat there all day long—and eventually raised $60!

29

GLOSSARY

confidence: believing in someone or something

confirm: to find to be true

divine: relating to, or coming from, a god

emancipate: to free from the control or power of another, usually referring to the freeing of slaves

hitch: to connect two things so that one moves another

immigrant: one who comes to a country to settle there

integrity: the quality of possessing high moral principles

racism: the belief that people of different races have different qualities and abilities and that some are superior or inferior

reap: to cut and gather a crop

smuggle: to take, bring, or carry somebody or something secretly into or out of a place

suffrage: the right to vote

unconscious: unable to see, hear, or sense what is happening because of accident or injury

Union: the side of the Northern states in the American Civil War

FOR MORE
Information

Books

Allen, Thomas B. *Harriet Tubman, Secret Agent: How Daring Slaves and Free Blacks Spied for the Union During the Civil War.* Washington, DC: National Geographic Society, 2006.

Waxman, Laura Hamilton. *How Did Slaves Find a Route to Freedom? And Other Questions About the Underground Railroad.* Minneapolis, MN: Lerner Classroom, 2011.

Websites

Harriet Tubman, Civil Rights Activist
www.biography.com/people/harriet-tubman-9511430
Read more about Harriet's life.

Harriet Tubman Historical Society
www.harriet-tubman.org
Explore a site dedicated to Harriet's life and achievements.

Underground Railroad
www.history.com/topics/black-history/underground-railroad
Learn the history of the Underground Railroad.

INDEX